# The
# CALLOUSED
# SOUL

## Uncovering *the*
## Real Woman Behind
## *the* Hardened Heart

# Evelyn Watkins

DESTINY IMAGE₀ PUBLISHERS, INC.
P.O. Box 310, Shippensburg, PA 17257-0310
*"Promoting Inspired Lives."*

This book and all other Destiny Image, Revival Press, MercyPlace, Fresh Bread, Destiny Image Fiction, and Treasure House books are available at Christian bookstores and distributors worldwide.

For a U.S. bookstore nearest you, call 1-800-722-6774.
For more information on foreign distributors, call 717-532-3040.
Reach us on the Internet: www.destinyimage.com.

ISBN 13 TP: 978-0-7684-0353-4
ISBN 13 Ebook: 978-0-7684-8483-0

For Worldwide Distribution, Printed in the U.S.A.
2 3 4 5 6 7 8 / 17 16 15 14 13

# *The*

# CALLOUSED

# SOUL

# CONTENTS

CHAPTER ONE

# THE STRONG AND RESILIENT

I remember watching television one day, and hearing a talk show host discuss the power of resilience. She spoke with such vigor of this characteristic which somehow was likened to a badge of honor to those who were able to overcome hardship. I remember thinking, "yeah, that's what I am...a strong, resilient overcomer. One who has endured much and has the strength and force to endure much more."

As I continued pondering that concept, I remember my pride quickly turned to disdain. Did I want to go through life wearing an armor of protection to forgo possible threats of attack? Had I been fooled to believe this saving grace of resilience would be a lifetime trophy to prove my ability to endure great tragedy?

I liken resilience to the heel of a foot. You know, if you didn't have shoes, and were to go outside barefoot, at first your foot would hurt. You'd probably bounce from heel to toe, foot to foot, in an attempt to protect your feet. However, after awhile, you would become accustomed to the discomfort. You'd walk around, perhaps grimacing all the while. After some time of this continued subjection to sharp objects, pebbles, and gravel, your foot would become hardened. It would begin to develop a callous; a hard, tough skin which would prevent harmful objects from penetrating the skin.

How wonderful God created our bodies; to know how to create a barrier of protection to assure foreign bodies can not enter in. But imagine if you then obtain a pair of sandals. You no longer have the need to walk barefoot, and you no longer have a biological need for that callous.

In light of this change, the callous now is merely an ugly, dried-up, hardened, dead-skinned nuisance, which no longer allows lotion or other necessary emollients to enter in. Notice the dichotomy. What first seemed to be a necessary bodily response to painful pressure is now a hindrance to the foot receiving the nourishment it needs to thrive, be supple, soft, and attractive.

I began to look at my life. Its tragedies, sorrows, shame... hardness. Then I began to observe how I had created a layer of protection, which once saved me, but now threatened my ability to experience meaningful intimacy with others because no one could really enter in. My soul was simply hard. Calloused. Unable to be penetrated. Unable to receive what I said I desperately wanted. Love.

You may look at this, surmise, and think, "well, I'm not hard; that doesn't really speak to any issue of mine." Let's ask ourselves a few key questions to see if perhaps we may need to work on removing dead skin from our own calloused heart.

### Question #1

Do you assume in general that people have a hidden agenda? *yes*

### Question #2

Do you have a difficult time meeting REAL people? *yes*

### Question #3

Would you say in general that you do not trust people? *yes*

### Question #4

Do you assume, men in particular, are hiding things from you? *yes*

### Question #5

Do you have difficulty with deep hugs, hand-holding, or any other non-sexual forms of touch with men or women? *no*

### Question #6

Are there things about yourself you will never tell anyone? *yes*

### Question #7

Do you ever feel afraid to tell people how you feel about them when discussing things like love? *yes*

### Question #8

Are you uncomfortable with others telling you that they love you? *yes*

### Question #9

Do you find yourself uncomfortable telling others you love them? *Sometimes*

### Question #10

When telling others you love them, do you prefer to say, "love you" rather than "I love you"? *love you*

### Question #11

Do you feel uncomfortable when receiving unexpected gifts from anyone not in your close circle of friends? *Yes*

### Question #12

Do you feel uncomfortable looking others in the eye and telling them of their significance in your life? *No*

### Question #13

Do you feel unsure as to how to respond when others compliment you excessively? *Yes*

### Question #14

Do you ever feel that when someone compliments you, they must have an ulterior motive? *Yes*

### Question #15

Do you ever feel obligated to give a gift to someone simply because they gave one to you? *Sometimes*

### Question #16

Do you ever question if your behavior was sensitive enough? *No*

### Question #17

Have you ever thought that perhaps everyone around you is much too sensitive? *Sometimes*

### Question #18

Do you have a difficult time forgiving? *No*

### Question #19

Do you put up an imaginary wall even after you've for-given someone for hurting you? *yes , sometimes*

> ♥ If you answered yes to less than five ques-tions, you probably have done a good job of maintaining a pliable heart

> ♥ If you answered yes to five or more ques-tions, you probably have developed imagi-nary layers on your heart which may have hindered healthy relationship development

The good news is, no matter how hard, just as you can see a trained professional who can use tools to remove the dead skin from the souls of your feet, we too, can use our tools to remove the hardness from our hearts.

I know with certainty if you will read this entire book, complete the tasks, and commit to change, you will discover a more loveable and loving woman who is meant for the Mas-ter's use!

Be certain to use the rear of this book to complete the series of activities to ensure your good success. You will love the woman you evolve into at the conclusion of all of the tasks! Enjoy the journey!

## Chapter Two

# Where Did It Begin?

Can you remember the day you told yourself to be strong? The day you realized you would have to toughen up or you would be swallowed alive by your life's circumstances?

I do. I was the sixth child in a family of nine. My mom and dad were very different people. My mother, a beautiful woman but sadly a schizophrenic, often drowned the voices which taunted her with alcohol. She was the disciplinarian: the one who executed judgment in our house. Her methods ranged depending on who you were and the issue at hand. My dad on the other hand seemed gentle and kind. I watched him push my mom around, so in my mind, he was stronger than she was. He could rescue me if I needed him. He was to me, my knight, my prince, my certainty of peace.

I remember being four years old and living on 66 Chandler Street. It was Christmas Eve in 1970. A few days earlier a social worker had visited and delivered presents for us all. Clothes, stuffed animals, and needful things we could only dream of having. Today, my mom and dad gave each of us one of the brand new, store-bought gifts. I received a beautiful quilted bathrobe, with rosebuds all over and pearl-like buttons. It was simply regal.

When I left my bedroom to use the bathroom, one of my sisters took my robe and hid it from me. When my mother asked for its whereabouts, I simply couldn't answer. My mother opened the hallway closet, tossed me inside, and quickly closed the door. I heard the padlock latch from the outside assuring that I could not leave. I had spent many hours, many days and nights in this closet. To a dwarf-like four-year-old, this pantry closet seemed to be quite large.

The closet held all of the canned and boxed USDA government food my family obtained freely each month. Whatever you desired, powdered eggs, powered milk, canned prunes, meat or peanut butter; lots of great things if you had knives for fingers. There were no snacks to be had or drinks to be drunk. I knew that if I were put in the closet in the morning I would be out by dinner. A dinner-time penalty would certainly mean at least the night's stay; that is, if my mother didn't forget I was there. To me, it was simply doing time. I learned how to do my time like a strong soldier. No tears. No whimpering. No whining. I didn't want my mother to know she could break me.

I listened as everyone marched to the kitchen for dinner. I couldn't tell what they were having for dinner. I imagined it was pork chops with gravy and rice. Mmmm. I imagined having a big cup of Kool-Aid. I was a bit hungry as I leaned against the wall with the doorknob at my head.

I continued to look at the shadows under the door and wondered why everyone was so quiet. They must have an awful lot of food. I brought my knees up to my chest and wrapped my arms around my legs. I nestled my small head on top of my wobbly knees. I talked out loud to myself and said, "I'm OK. I'm not going to cry."

Suddenly, I heard a wave of laughter. "Daddy, shake more, more Daddy." I knew that Daddy was making popcorn. It was a sight to see. With the oil hot and the popcorn ready, Daddy would begin to shake his whole body as he moved the pot back and forth. I began to feel sorry for myself. It was cold in the closet so I pulled my brother's t-shirt over my knees to cover my little legs and part of my ankles. I wondered if there were any other children spending Christmas Eve in a closet, cold with a thin worn t-shirt. I comforted myself by imagining that Santa Claus could come and rescue me.

"Line up!" I heard Mommy call. I knew they would be going to watch television for a while. I had hoped that I would get to see Rudolph the Red-Nosed Reindeer. I watched the shadows under the door and guessed which set of foot shadows belonged to whom. I played that game until they were all clear out of sight, in the den.

I nestled my head into my knees. At thirty-nine pounds, I was quite small for my age. I had little pencil legs and spaghetti arms. My head was the largest part of my body; well, that and my belly. I heard a scratch. I hated the scratching sounds. I was quite acquainted with the apartment's rats. My sister Pebbs and I used to make believe they were kittens. Sometimes when we rested under the bed where we slept, we could hear them trying to travel through the walls. Tonight, I was a little scared. The closet was so dark. So very dark. I put my hand in front of my eyes to see if I could see my fingers. I couldn't. The scratching continued and then seemed to suddenly stop. If only I could reach the string hanging from the light bulb above, I could turn on the light.

I heard the faintest leap from one can to the next. Then a quiet gnawing. I thought, "maybe the *kitty* will eat all of the powdered eggs and I won't have to eat any more."

I began to grow weary. The hairs on my little body standing on end from both the cold air and fear. I began to feel a welling within my little body. I didn't like that feeling. Then a sharp urge. I had to use the bathroom.

My options in the closet were few. I could do my best to endure the unbearable pain until morning, and hope that my mother would let me out at dawn. Or, I could relieve my bladder, sit in the pool of urine, and then face a beating with the extension cord in the morning when Mommy opened the door and saw the disgrace.

I just held my little body all the more tighter and told myself, "I am OK. I will not cry." I may have fallen asleep as I continually dozed dreamily, but the incessant gnawing seemed to keep me awake.

I heard my brothers and sisters saying goodnight as they headed to their bedrooms. I felt the darting pain in my little abdomen. "I wonder if it's close to morning yet?" I asked myself. The pain was so excruciating. I felt as though someone were stepping on my belly with the spiked shoes football men would wear. I told myself, "I am OK. I will not cry." The light from the den was turned off. Until now, that very faint and distant shadow seemed to provide some light in this great darkness. Now, I sat gripping my knees with my legs crossed enduring the stabbing pressure in my belly. My lower back began to ache as I exercised my bladder.

The pain seemed to be magnified as the gnawing was amplified. It seemed so loud in the closet; so loud in the darkness. Just then, I heard a familiar melody. It was my Daddy whistling a favorite Sam Cooke tune. I began smiling to myself. I couldn't help it. "See, you were OK. There was no need to cry!" I told myself. Daddy was the best intervention. He was so strong and he wasn't at all afraid of Mommy. My goodness, I had seen him knock her down with one hand. Mommy did whatever Daddy said. He was in charge. He was the boss. And he loved me.

My excitement was threatening my clean panties. I had to remain calm although it was hard. I knew just as soon as I called out to Daddy that he would let me out and would certainly let me sleep in my own room under April's bed for Christmas Eve.

Suddenly, I saw the light under the door. Daddy had turned on the hallway light as he approached the kitchen. My heart began to race with excitement. I put my cheek to the floor so I was certain to catch him just as he got to the closet. I wanted to whisper to assure that I didn't wake my mother. I stared at the light under the door. Somehow that small light seemed to flood the whole closet. I turned my head and saw the cause of all of the gnawing. He sat perched in a gnawed-out box of powdered eggs, just as I had hoped.

My heart continued to leap as my dad happily whistled down the hall. Just as his shadow approached the door, my fist, the size of a small plum tapped on the door just as gently as it could. "Daddy..." I called. My dad stopped in his tracks. I knew he was right in front of the door because the light was obstructed with his shadow. "Daddy, can you let me out, I have to use the bathroom?"

I stood up with one hand firmly in between my legs to help my holding efforts and the other hand placed eagerly on the doorknob. "Baby," dad replied, "I can't let you out...your mother, she'll be real mad." His words were like the resounding noise you hear after you clap cymbals together. They simply continued to resonate in my ears... "I can't let you out...I can't let you out...I can't let you out."

"But Daddy, I have to go really bad. I, I don't think I can hold...." I saw his shadow disappear in the middle of my sentence. He simply walked away. Vanished.

I, still standing with one hand on the doorknob and the other firmly between my legs, made my most valiant attempt to say, "I am OK. I will not...." But before the words could be mouthed, I felt the warmth of urine spill quickly on my thighs. The dripping sound on the wood floor seemed to echo. I thought quickly of my tomorrow: of the beating with the extension cord; of the concurrent sentence in the closet. I wondered why my father hated me so. Why wasn't I loveable? Why wouldn't he want to rescue me? He was bigger and stronger than Mommy.

My feet stood wet and now cold by my bodily fluids. I shivered and rubbed my hands over my goose-bumped arms.

I attempted to say again, "I am OK. I will not cry." Just then, I tasted the salty excretions from my own eyes. Having failed every imprisoned promise to myself, I bellowed in anguish as tears fiercely fell, covering my face.

As I moaned quietly, my Daddy happily whistled as he returned back to his bedroom. He stopped at the closet and listened. Hearing my pitiful whimpers, he asked, "Baby, are you OK?" I, refusing to let him know my discontent, with a firm and undaunted voice said, "Yes, Daddy, I am OK."

After that experience, I learned to control my bladder. I learned that crouching very small and breathing short, faint breaths will help maintain body heat. I learned that a beating on Christmas Day is not so bad. I learned that concurrent sentences in the closet were not the end of the world. More importantly, I learned that my Daddy was not so strong after all. He was not my knight in shining armor, a prince, or a savior. He was just a frail man; flawed and unworthy of the pedestal I had carved in my heart. He did not rescue me that night and he would never rescue me. Although he didn't hit like Mommy, his bruises scarred much deeper. Although he was stronger than Mommy, he somehow seemed so weak now; and now I learned for the first time that I needed to be much stronger. I would survive this and many other lessons in lonely dark places.

My first life lesson on tenacity was learned in the dark, by the light under the door. That lesson in the closet was a defining moment for me. It became a memorable map I would use to connect the dots of my journey. It was followed by much physical, emotional, and verbal abuse; not to mention multiple assaults of molestation.

You can understand why it became very easy for me to develop an apathetic attitude toward friends, family, and others. It was much easier to have acquaintances than friends. Easier to find fault in family members, which would offer me further justification for maintaining distant relationships with relatives.

Just as I had done in that closet, declaring that I wouldn't cry. Believing no one could hurt me. Determined to not allow my mother to break me. I played that same message throughout adolescence and adulthood.

You too, may have had a defining moment. A final straw that told you, "no more!" It was a place where you realized that people could swallow you up. Perhaps you believed that men were destined to hurt you. Cheat. Lie. Steal. Manipulate.

It could be abuse, neglect, betrayal, or abandonment. Who knows? But I do know that your moment changes you. It makes you different. For some of us, it hardens us. Like that foot, earlier described, it takes a soft and supple heart, and layers it with hurt, pain, disappointment, and mistrust; which later is unattractive, dead, and hardened.

I found myself observing other people and wondering how they made it through life being so sensitive. Being moved by every emotional whim. Falling apart at the knowledge of someone being sick. Overtly ecstatic at the announcement of someone's pregnancy. "Get a grip," I'd think! But what I discovered was that there was nothing wrong with them. Instead there was something wrong with me.

The soul of a woman is her "feeler." It is where her mind and emotions lie. Imagine going through the world and your sense of touch was gone. How would you know if you felt something sharp or prickly? How would you be able to feel the pleasure of a warm bubble bath?

Can you see how the inability to feel properly hinders you from discerning real pleasure and legitimate pain? Do you really want to live a life without being able to truly feel? Many think they'd rather feel nothing than to feel any pain. What a tragedy.

The concept of no pain is where I deliberately resided for many, many years. Having developed hardness as my armor of protection, I simply participated in my life rather than richly experiencing it. It wasn't until I developed a real awareness of who God was did I come to learn that I would never be able to share the freshness of this divine love, absent of my ability to be emotionally moved by others. The Amplified Bible states the following:

> *For we do not have a High Priest Who is unable to understand and sympathize and have a shared feeling with our weaknesses and infirmities and liability to the assaults of temptation...* (Hebrews 4:15).

I am convinced that like Genesis 1:26, I am made in God's image and God's likeness. Thus, I am like God. And because I am like Him, I should be one who is able to understand and sympathize.

The King James says, "touched" with the feelings and weaknesses of others. To be touched implies one can be moved emotionally. This charge is impossible to one whose heart is closed off to others. Whose armor of strength is wrapped around their heart like a cocoon.

I realized I had to embrace the process of tearing away at my hardened heart. Breaking apart each layer by doing the following:

1. acknowledging the pain

2. identifying the source

3. assessing the damage

4. forgiving those who had hurt me

5. witness a better model

6. sow my desire in others

7. be willing to be vulnerable and begin again

This won't be any easy process, but a necessary one if you are to get the love you deserve; the love you say you want. The love you were created to give.

# CHAPTER THREE

# ACKNOWLEDGING THE PAIN

The human body is a fascinating and complex demonstration of the self-sufficiency for which we are fashioned. It knows how to hold on to fat storage when you don't feed it, it knows how to eliminate waste, and it has been created with a warning system and a mechanism to heal itself. Like the opening analogy of the calloused foot, our entire body is made to warn of potential trouble and then follow with appropriate action to heal itself. I said earlier that our soul (feeler, holder of our emotions) is likened to this analogy.

The seven steps that I listed to tear away at the hardened heart is a generic prescription for any emotional offense that may have left the scar of callousness. The goal is wholeness. Not just healing, but wholeness.

I recall having a small topical sebaceous tumor on my back and stomach. I discovered the tumor on my back when my bra strap rubbed against it and I would feel a sharp pain. Using a second mirror I examined my back, contacted a surgeon, and had the tumor removed. The surgeon then assessed whether the tumor was benign or malignant. Of course I had great joy to learn that it was merely a fatty tumor growing on a bed of nerves. However, to my dismay, the two-inch incision the doctor made to remove this unwanted nuisance left a gaping scar. That tumor was removed twenty years ago, and yet the scar still remains.

Had the tumor been cancerous and any further treatment deemed necessary, although the outcome would have been successful, the scar still would have remained. What does this all mean? It is the difference between merely being healed and being whole. Healing means the intrusion, the disease has ceased to exist. Wholeness implies there is no evidence that the intrusion or disease ever occurred.

My desire is that we all would be able to progress through the process of wholeness, tearing away the evidence of hardness that our emotional intrusions have left behind. That when others look upon us, they would not be able to see any evidence of our previous pain. No scars of our painful past and no dead skin to hinder us from wearing the now beautiful sandals set aside for our adornment.

## MY PAINFUL DISCOVERY

Ever notice how often people use phrases like, "I don't care" or the more contemporary version, "whatever." These are code words for, "I choose not to let you in," "I will not be disappointed," or "I will not be hurt." They are very effective in shutting people out and shutting communication down. Problem is, how exactly are we to get the love we want or effectively love others if our approach to love is "whatever?" Does that mean, "whatever love you send God, I'll take." Or, "whatever type of emotionally bankrupt relationship comes my way is OK with me." Or how about, "I don't care if you attempt to overtake me with kindness, sincerity, and thoughtfulness. Your overtures are irrelevant."

Of course when we examine this phraseology, it seems irrational that anyone would respond in this manner, however, our daily experiences demonstrate that these conditioned responses make up our most effective arsenal. Actually, they were part of my regular repertoire, which I have to occasionally harness my lips from repeating.

So what is your conditioned response? When did you begin that inner dialogue which shut others out in order to guard your heart? When did you begin to say, "I don't care?" These code words should tell us that pain is present. It can be tough to acknowledge it exists because you may have done a great job of covering it up. Remember, tender footsteps to the ground and initial pain is eventually overwhelmed by continued exposure. Eventually, you no longer can feel it. My personal challenge was to uncover the root of my nonchalant, cavalier attitude.

## MY ROOT

My mom was hospitalized when I was six years old. She slipped into a coma and remained in a vegetative state until 1987, when she died at age forty-seven. My Aunt Eunice and Uncle Wilbur took care of me and my brother Scott following my mom's hospitalization. On June 10, 1973, I turned seven and my Aunt Eunice had baked my very first cake.

There was to be no fanfare, no friends over or the like, but a wonderful celebration of me. It was a first. She hummed through the house as she prepared lunch and set the bright beautiful packages on the dining room table. This experience was indeed a contrast from the forgotten birthdays with my own natural mother. I don't know if it was the oppression of her mental illness, personal poverty, or simply a disdain for unnecessary functions such as parties but such childhood festivities were not an early memory.

But this day, I was remembered. In fact, my aunt went through the trouble to discover that my birthday was not the day my mom had listed in school records and the like, but in fact was eleven days earlier. My aunt was the kind of woman who had cookies and milk waiting for you when you came home from school. She oozed "momminess" and was unapologetic in her actions.

The day was set and all was well...wonderful in fact. It was just about lunchtime when my Uncle Wilbur returned home and had a guest with him. Who was it? Was it the person he was yelling at on the telephone earlier? Yes, actually it was. It was my father. He looked a little battered with help from my Uncle Wilbur. Seems he wasn't too interested in showing up for my birthday lunch so my Uncle thought he would provide some encouragement.

He awkwardly attempted to offer well wishes and made some excuse for forgetting my birthday. "Who cares?" I thought. He never remembered my birthday. His tousled hair and bruised face only reminded me how forgettable I was. More importantly, he demonstrated that it would take a brawl to bring about a forced birthday blessing which obviously was insincere.

On June 10, 1975, I was in fourth grade at Woodland Street Elementary School. I was living with my second foster parent who was a single twenty-five-year-old woman. My foster mom was not the kind of woman who allowed neighborhood or school friends to come to her home.

In fact, I lived with her for six years and never had a friend over to visit. She did the best she knew considering she had no children. She was not one to forget purchasing a gift but was not the kind to fool with the silliness of cakes, balloons, and the like. Knowing this, you can imagine my joy during fourth grade.

My fourth grade teacher, Mrs. Adamitis, was tall with mousy brown hair and a long nose with a bump in the middle. She wasn't a particularly striking woman and she didn't have a memorable personality. But she did have a wonderful array of activities she used to engage and celebrate the children in her class. My favorite: birthday celebrations.

In Mrs. Adamitis's class, birthdays meant something. You see, on the student's birthday, she'd have a child request the company of the birthday child to the water fountain. When they left, we'd turn out the lights, and Mrs. Adamitis would take out a Drakes Cake cupcake with one candle, and a specially purchased story from the "Golden Book" collection. Obviously these two items may have cost little more than a dollar at the time. But the celebration was about your peers treating you special all day, singing happy birthday to you, and knowing your teacher chose a book that you personally would love.

Well, Friday, June 10, 1975, was my birthday. I watched this birthday process all year long. Student after student relish in this time of honor and celebration. Today was the last day of school. It would be all about me. I looked in the mirror a few extra minutes: checked my two pigtails, made sure I had Vaseline on my lips and knees, and wiped my dress shoes. I wanted to look as dreamy as I felt.

I couldn't stop beaming when I got to school. I couldn't imagine who she would use to lure me from the classroom. As the hours dragged on, my anticipation escalated. School dismissed at 3:00 and it was 1:30 and no water fountain break, no cupcake, no book. Could it be? Could she have forgotten my birthday?

I confided in my friend Elani Karkaseni. I shared my hurt and disappointment. She offered some leftover snack in her lunchbox. I said no, I wasn't hungry. I wanted my celebration, my book, and my song. We lined up for a farewell program in the auditorium. After we found our seats, I saw Elani telling Mrs. Adamitis that she forgot my birthday. She looked over at me a bit distraught and I simply turned away. She then coasted to the music director and whispered something in her ear.

After the final announcements and pronouncement of summer vacation, the music teacher spoke gleefully into the microphone, "There's a special girl who we need to remember with a very special song. Join me as we sing Happy Birthday to Evelyn." And there you go, the song was sung. Yet, it did not change the fact that I indeed was forgotten.

If I had not underscored this experience in my life, it would be very easy to allow myself to become someone's afterthought. A forgotten item on someone's checklist. I did what I always did which was pretend that I didn't care. Lie and tell my friends that I had some over-the-top birthday party with every imaginable gift a kid could want. The truth was, I figured out that I really wasn't important. Not a priority and not worth the trouble of a cupcake and a book.

You see, for me, it wasn't about the value of my teacher's gifts. Frankly I'm sure my foster mom would have given me something that valued at least the stipend the Department of Social Services gave for a child's birthday ($15.00). It was the value of celebration. The joy of hearing my peers rejoice in me. The thunderous laughter, the "make a wish" shouts. The value of someone remembering not because they were given a stipend or felt a sense of obligation but simply because the object of their remembrance was also the object of their affection.

I remember the first time I read Psalms 8:4 with disbelief: *What is man, that thou art mindful of him? And the son of man, that thou visitest him?*

It penetrated my heart like a fine scalpel. That the creator of the universe was mindful of me. I, Evelyn, was on His mind. He had the world to manage, yet He still pondered me.

Sometimes when we hear the truth concerning the Creator's affinity toward us, we expect an immediate transformation. Not so. Even now, I am quite nonchalant concerning my own birthday, Mother's Day, Christmas, and the like. I never projected my weak expectations onto others, however, I can be cynical concerning the relevance of such days. This response is merely an effort to cover up the truth; being forgotten hurts.

Moreover, my true growth had to come as others reached out to me. There have been many over the years who have displayed their love and generosity toward me through gifts, honorary events, or most difficult for me, written notes. As these sentiments were extended, I had great difficulty receiving them. I had become a very generous giver, which was critical for my wholeness (I will explain in a later chapter), but still wasn't able to receive the love and affirmation I needed because I had told myself that I didn't care about people, what they thought of me, or if they thought of me at all. This was a source of pain for me and hence, an important experience to learn from. I would not grow from mere reflection but acknowledgment. My acknowledgment would begin as a result of writing. Thus the process begins.

# CHAPTER FOUR

# WRITE IT DOWN

I discovered the process of writing. There is something so very powerful about writing; much more so than speaking alone. Writing not only allows you the ability to ponder a message in your mind but then translates it on an eternal stone of sorts. A stone which you have to witness with your own eyes; one which you can peruse over and over again.

The written word indeed is quite strong. I remember beginning the writings of a novel many years ago. I had spoken of these childhood experiences numerous times; some of which I had spoken of in conference settings. Yet, when I began writing the same experiences down on paper, the words seem to bite. They were sharp and painful. For the first time in my life I was seeing my most tragic experiences on paper and witnessing the words there was like being a voyeur to my own life.

I was stunned at my response; my sudden rush of grief. Where did this come from? It was merely the written word evoking hidden emotions which had hardened over time.

I encourage you, before you read another chapter, to do just that. Give yourself the opportunity to consider the very first offense. The very first time someone hurt, betrayed, or disappointed you. The time that you learned you'd have to pretend you were OK, just to be around your offender.

Or maybe the time you forced yourself not to cry when you hurt so deeply, you thought you could vomit. Maybe it was the day you pretended not to notice people looking at your scar or your oversized body. Maybe it was the day you saw your name in the paper under the divorces published. Or maybe it was having a cynical parent who thought that celebrating the juvenile experiences like birthdays, Valentine's, and the like was fool's play.

Now write it down. The first moment will help uncover the instances that followed. Commit to write it down. Writing is validating its existence. The validation doesn't extend power but instead allots you a focal point to direct your new power.

After you write down the first item (perhaps you only have one) describe your statement of truth which affirms why it was wrong. I turned to the Bible for verses which provided me with truth and support. I began with Mark 9:35-37; as it addresses how Jesus respected and loved children.

Oftentimes, we want justice. We want the person who has hurt us to first acknowledge that what they did or failed to do was wrong. Unfortunately, many of us don't get that luxury. Because we are made like God, and He is a God of justice, we yearn for the same. Therefore, your statement of truth has to provide you the justice your offender cannot. It should affirm the wrongness of the offender and help bring peace to you. This very activity has done the same for me.

Once you complete this exercise, use that statement or Bible verse as a mantra to live by. Allow it to be the statement you put in your wallet, on your mirror in the bathroom, on your refrigerator, and most importantly on your tongue. This is the first and second step to you uncovering your vulnerable heart.

# CHAPTER FIVE

# DO THE WORK

So by now you should have written at least one experience which was a defining moment. You may have many or perhaps just one. My first defining moment was the light under the door. It was my first life message. That is what the moment is, a message that offers insight to who you are and what you are supposed to be. My first message was: no one is going to protect you and the second was: you are forgettable. Those moments became life messages which told me who I was and what I was to be.

What have you discovered as your defining moment and/ or life message? Now that you know what it is, you must give yourself the permission to feel the feeling. Acknowledging that moment, the pain, knowing the root of the pain is the first part of the work. I've had many experiences which when grouped together seemed like one big assault of abuse on my physical and spiritual body. Unfortunately, those kinds of experiences can really muddy the water and make it difficult to understand oneself and one's weakness.

One mistake I see so many women make is to assume that you can simply pray away your pain. Or more commonly, "wait" away your pain. Time really does lessen the edge of our hurt but time alone will not heal. Just as cancer left untreated does not heal itself with time, likewise, pain left alone will not be healed by time. Pain has a purpose. It lets the mind know that there is something wrong. Imagine bleeding internally and yet you feel no discomfort, displeasure, or pain. You would surely die. The same is true for our soul.

I remember being a new mom and bathing my daughter Gabrielle. She was probably about eight months old at the time. She was splashing and enjoying her bubble bath when I noticed something in the tub. She had a bowel movement in the tub. Witnessing her stool floating there in the tub brought a disturbing memory to mind. I recalled being in the bathtub with my younger sister and a similar situation arose. My mother noted that one of us defecated in the bathtub.

After questioning us both to determine who made the mess in the tub, my mother was enraged at our dual denial. She proceeded to push my sister's head under the water. As her body jerked violently, I belted out loud, "I did it!" With one quick backhand, my head then hit the tub and then all went black. It was a very quick memory which I recalled in just a brief moment while Gabrielle happily splashed in the tub. I began to weep. It was the first opportunity I had to grieve the pain I had endured as a little girl. It was all so real, so clear. I wanted to wail like a baby but I had to pull it together. My husband saw me and questioned if my tears were because I was overwhelmed by my daughter's accident. I told him no, just feeling bad for myself.

And that's what I did. I took a few minutes to simply feel bad for myself, and it was OK. I mean, who else was going to feel bad for that little girl? Who is going to cry for her? So I did. I cried for that little girl. I then wrote down how it felt. I expressed my anger over it. I wondered how someone could do that to their baby girl? I felt the injustice of it all. And then it passed.

You have to really dig deep; feel the feeling and then allow it to pass. Do not make the mistake of expecting others to understand your injustice. People may not rally behind you on this and it's OK. Sometimes we yearn for the validation of others to demonstrate that what we endured was real or that somehow it mattered. It's not necessary for others to validate that. You know how you felt when others referred to you as the "big one," the "dark one," the "fast one." You know how it felt to be rejected for another woman, overlooked again and again even though you were the more qualified employee. You don't have to get anyone on your side to agree that it happened, that it hurt, or that it was real.

Some ask, how long should I feel bad about this? Well, that varies depending on the individual. I would say, don't allow this focused grieving process to drag on for longer than a month. Keep in mind, we're not referring to something that just happened today, we're talking about something that happened perhaps a long time ago. You have to use your own discernment. But we're merely allowing ourselves time to acknowledge and feel the pain. This is not a funeral. Just the grieving process. I reflect on these Bible verses to support the relevance of my own grief. The Bible says this:

*...Weeping may endure for a night, but joy comes in the morning* (Psalms 30:5 AMP).

There is a season of weeping and grieving but God expects for you to know that eventually the season should end. Joy does come in the morning. It comes with the light and the newness of day.

> *A time to weep and a time to laugh, a time to mourn, and a time to dance* (Ecclesiastes 3:4 AMP).

Another great lesson the book of Psalms offers is this:

> *The Lord nigh unto them that are of a broken heart; and saveth such as be of a contrite spirit* (Psalm 34:18).

I used to believe, like many others, that if I seemed hurt, broken, or disappointed, then somehow I must not have real faith. If I prayed properly, I wouldn't feel such pain. Don't make this tragic mistake. As you can see from this Scripture, the Lord is near them which have a broken heart. Let's not confuse the concept. God does relish the hour we come to Him broken and realizing our deep need for Him. He is not relishing in your brokenness, but you realizing your need for Him. As parents, we don't get excited that our children get hurt, but we do relish in the joy of them coming to us for comfort. That never changes no matter how old they become.

Remember, grieving is part of the journey, it is not a destination. We don't live a life of black cloaks and ashes, somber, but know that God is near you during this season and people of faith *do* experience brokenness.

CHAPTER SIX

# ASSESSING THE DAMAGE: DEVELOPING YOUR EMOTIONAL RESUME

Now that you've done the work of exploring the source of your pain and acknowledging it, you have to really give thought to the complexity of how it has changed you. This is where the great cloak of denial sets in. People of faith, in particular, oftentimes believe that if they are in fact spiritually renewed, somehow they are divorced from their past. Keep in mind, even in divorcement, the relationship you had with the other person does not disappear when the judge signs the decree.

We are still the sum of our life experiences, the harvest of our past. If we want to create a better future, established on better promises, we must assess the damage our past has created.

I remember speaking to a man (we'll call him David) whose wife was unfaithful during their marriage. It hurt him deeply. The couple went through counseling together but were unable to save their marriage. He began dating another woman who was really quite remarkable. She was everything he suggested he wanted in a woman. Beautiful, smart, self-sufficient, and outgoing. The problem: he was extremely insecure about her work relationships with other men. She conducted herself in a professional manner with unwavering character. Her stellar integrity unfortunately wasn't good enough. His irrational demands for her professional isolation began to threaten the seedling of a fulfilling relationship.

See even though he acknowledged his pain and clearly knew the source, he had underestimated how much it had changed him. He did not recognize that he needed much more than just counseling. He needed more than prayer. He needed to come to terms with the unconscious transformation he had made. This is not new age ideology. This is simply seed time and harvest time. It acknowledges that when something is planted in your life, it brings fruit after its kind. This gentlemen's behavior is not exceptional; it is in fact the fruit after its kind.

> *And God said, "Let the earth bring forth grass, the herb yielding seed, and the fruit tree yielding fruit after his kind, whose seed is in itself, upon the earth: and it was so"* (Genesis 1:11).

We will discuss this more extensively later, but the message here is that our behavior should not be a surprise to us. It is merely the fruit (the expected outcome) of a prior behavior, or experience (seed).

David had much work to do before he was emotionally and spiritually equipped for a healthy committed relationship. Likewise, the woman whose heart he was fetching could not appreciate how ill-prepared David was for a new relationship or marriage.

I'm sure you can examine your life and find areas where you were changed because of an event or experience. Loss of a child, divorce, abuse, unfaithfulness, termination, disease, betrayal, or even winning the lottery. These events undoubtedly make a mark on your life which is not automatically erased. There has to be a deliberate effort to change the *change*.

I struggled with my weight throughout my adolescence. I can clearly remember seventh grade when the school nurse had all of the girls line up and she'd check your height, weight, and your spine for scoliosis. I could hear the girls before me talk back and forth about their ninety-something weight. Next would be my turn. I'm certain I was never ninety anything; perhaps in fifth grade.

"Evelyn, step up." I was always stocky and possessed a bit of an athletic build so even the nurse underestimated my weight. I was mortified that she had to push the top marker to the one hundred pound mark. Then pound by pound; she moved the lever. Really, she didn't skip five at a time, just one slow agonizing pound at a time. She moved the lower marker until it reached 131. That was my weight...131. As I passed my friends who were still standing in line, they of course asked me, "whatdaya weigh, Ev?" "Ninety nine," I said quickly.

As the years passed, my untruthful answer increased by the slightest of margins. Secretly, I tried different fad diets. I remember one when I was in sixth grade. Seven bananas one day, seven hotdogs another, seven eggs another, and seven oranges on the last. You were supposed to lose about ten pounds in the four days. I don't recall how successful I was, but I do know that it didn't last for long.

My problem wasn't the quantity of food I ate. Instead, I secretly binged on sweets, soda, and candy then pretended in front of others that my steadily increasing weight was a physiological wonder. My ever-abundant body was hiding a deeper fear and shame. It would remain hidden until I was nineteen years old. After the T.O.P.S. program, Gloria Stevens (circa 1980), Weight Watchers, and Richard Simmons, I came to realize my problem wasn't my insatiable hunger. But I certainly was hungry. My challenge wasn't even my hidden addiction, although I was hiding.

Take a look at this: "He reveals the deep and secret things; He knows what is in the darkness, and the light dwells with Him!" (Dan. 2:22 AMP).

Not only did God know what I was doing in the dark, He knew why I did it and He knew the *change* that changed me. Although I hated my oversized body, I loved that it made me invisible. It allowed me, I believed, to go unnoticed. It was my hiding place. It wasn't until I came to realize that my body was a form of armor for me, could I then do the real work to remove it.

Why did I need this armor? What was I hiding? Well, I was hiding my body. My sexually enticing body. My curvaceous figure was daunted with titles like Bertha Butt or Chesty Morgan. I knew very young that this body was no friend of mine. It invited unrestrained animalistic gestures which I was powerless to control.

I was a foster child who was not covered (protected) by any father figure and not easily believed. The neighborhood pizza maker fondled me at age ten. My foster mother's brother had sodomized me by age eleven. By age thirteen, her live-in boyfriend chased me through the apartment, threatening the same; all the while knowing my complaints would not be credible. By nineteen, the last overture came from a pastor, who took the liberty to grope my buttocks during a friendly hug of thanks.

As a foster child who aged out of the system, I was placed in four different homes. At each departure, I would lose something. A Snoopy telephone that I thought was a gift to me, I soon discovered was only a gift if I lived in THAT home. A small television: only a gift in THAT home. Bedding: only a Christmas gift in THAT home.

What I knew for sure was that in this world, the only thing that was truly mine was my body. It was mine. When I moved from place to place, it went with me. Yet, I really did not possess power over it at all. My weakness...my vulnerability, was my lack of covering. No protection. No one to guard me. My only hope was to be invisible. Unappealing, unattractive, and unwanted. How did sexual abuse change me? It covered up the outgoing, talkative, self-assured girl with a young woman whose body became her covering. Her hiding place.

I can recall walking downtown after being "touched" by this man of God. I remember thinking, maybe those men who assaulted me as a young girl weren't evil. Maybe there was something wrong with me. I knew of no one who had this history of older men attempting such assaults. And this guy, he was a pastor...why would he feel safe and secure with such impropriety? I must be giving some sort of wicked signal. There truly must be something on me. I was always the kind of kid, the kind of woman, who was very conscious and verbal about my circumstances.

Because I could flippantly describe to friends the hardships I endured, I really felt as though I was handling it. I didn't have control necessarily, but I was strong enough to handle it. It wasn't going to break me. Remember that line?

But God showed me myself for the first time that day. This day, as I questioned out loud during my thirty-minute walk, the answers leaped in my heart at the same time. It was as though I were in a counseling session and someone was speaking clearly. "You were touched because you were easy. Predators recognize easy prey. You were a child with no covering. No one was really looking out for you. You were no one's daughter. No one ever feared that you would tell, or that you'd be believed. You were the perfect object for violation. This pastor knew you would never tell your foster mother, therefore, again you were an easy object to violate."

I went from disappointment in this man I had come to trust to anger. For the first time, I really felt angry. I didn't feel like a victim. I didn't feel like a child. I felt like a woman who knew she was blameless. I knew I did nothing wrong and I knew there was nothing wrong with me. I knew my body was not a lure that a grown man could not resist. Surely a grown man could choose to do the right thing. But I also knew my body was not the hiding place I hoped it was.

All of the quick weight-loss endeavors could not compete with the revelation of that moment. I no longer had to hide. People ask me oftentimes, "How did you lose the weight?" I empathize with their desperation to know. I know how that feels. I know how it feels to buy every one of the magazines with the latest diet on its cover in hopes that this time, it's really going to work. I know how it feels to be captive in a body you don't believe you deserve and don't understand how you got there. I really understand the desperation in the eyes of women who look at their thinner counterparts and think, "is it the diet soda, yogurt, or the meatless diet?" But the truth is diets didn't work for me.

I had to change my "*change*." Abuse changed me. And a diet wasn't going to change me back. Truth was going to change me. And the truth was, I wasn't doing an effective job hiding myself. Emotionally, I was hidden. But physically, predators still saw my vulnerability. They saw someone who had no one to tell. No protection and no covering. My peers still saw a young girl who had no control over the only asset she owned. Herself.

So how did I lose the weight? I lost my *change*. I rejected the idea that I had to continue the same story in these new chapters of my life. Food was no longer a tool in my arsenal to cover me up; instead it was my fuel to strengthen me. I discovered that as I hungered and craved for my bingefest of Entenmann's chocolate chip cookies, Twizzlers licorice, and Schweppes Ginger Ale, I could thwart off my pangs with spiritual food and truly be satisfied.

As you ponder how you get to your "*change,*" ponder this challenge from Haggai 1:6-7 in the Amplified Bible.

> *You have sown much, but you have reaped little; you eat, but you do not have enough; you drink, but you do not have your fill; you clothe yourselves, but no one is warm; and he who earns wages has earned them to put them in a bag with holes in it.*

> *Thus says the Lord of hosts: Consider your ways (your previous and present conduct) and how you have fared.*

Insatiable hunger for food: consider your ways. Always needing someone to affirm you: consider your ways. Insecure or jealous: consider your ways. Addicted to pornography: consider your ways.

This verse is so telling because it affirms the truth, which is you can already possess everything you need, yet you engage the world as though you lack something. And you very well may, but the only way you'll discover what you lack is to consider *your previous and present conduct and how you have fared.*

It seems like a lifetime ago since I struggled with my weight. Shortly after I gave birth to my daughter, Gabrielle, I put my wholeness to the test and passed. Ten stress-free months after she was born, I was right back to my pre-birth weight of 120 pounds. It wasn't a fight, it wasn't a struggle, it simply was honoring the *change* that I had *changed.*

My advice to David was to take some time to assess his damage. To really discover how the failure and betrayal of his marriage had altered his confidence in women. How that same failure left him feeling insecure concerning his ability to be enough for the woman God had for him. I challenged him to consider how the infidelity may pose unreasonable expectations upon another woman.

Up until that point, David really thought that his new love could do things that would help him heal, like say: call him frequently from work, avoid all conversations with men, and transfer accounts with male clients to others. His new lady friend really tried to accommodate him, which was a mistake. It was not her responsibility to help him experience wholeness. He had to do that on his own. This bruise would feel like a yoke around her neck their entire marriage if he didn't master it.

I believe many times we do a disservice to others by not allowing them to really consider how their previous conduct or experiences have changed them. We can over-spiritualize the process of becoming whole and miss the tangible part of the work. Whether divorce or job loss, the impact on us is relevant and affects the way we engage future relationships of all sorts.

I don't believe people should be able to marry, have children, or enter into a legal business partnership without first pondering an Emotional Resume. Your Emotional Resume should state your mission statement and your goals. Then it should ask a series of questions: What have you experienced? What have you learned from the experience? How long and long ago was the experience? What education or training have you acquired that now equips you for this new position of mother, father, wife, husband, or business partner? Who can we contact (references) to verify your stability and truthfulness concerning your emotional competency?

Let's start by reviewing several assessment statements and see if any apply to you. If you find that the statement is applicable, follow the numbered statement with, "how has this changed me?"

1. Discovered you were adopted

2. Won a large sum of money

3. Parent or loved one has become physically disabled

4. Parent was an alcoholic or drug user

5.   Parents divorced

6.   Abused as a child or as an adult

7.   Started drinking as a teen

8.   Had a promiscuous lifestyle

9.   Contracted an STD

10.  Partner or spouse was unfaithful

11.  Loved one died

12.  You or loved one have fatal disease

13.  Had an abortion

14.  Committed a felony

15.  Lost your job

16.  Lost custody of your children

17.  Falsely accused of some wrongdoing

18.  Lost your home

19.  Filed bankruptcy

20.  Sued

21.  Abandoned

22.  Discovered your spouse was gay

If none of these statements apply to you, it should at least give you a starting point of what to consider. Remember, we are trying to assess the damage or impact our experience has left and it starts with the catalyst that brought about our *change*. Here's a passage to ponder from Ecclesiastes 3:15 in the Amplified Bible:

> *That which is now already has been, and that which is to be already has been; and God seeks that which has passed by [so that history repeats itself].*

The verse teaches us that history repeats itself unless we begin another story, so let's begin. Our story will start with a sound Personal Resume. A resume is a tool job seekers use to convey to a potential employer that they are competent, experienced, and trained for the position they seek to fill. Many people have multiple resumes because they seek multiple classifications of jobs. Likewise, you should have a resume for each type of position you desire. Want to be married (again)? Your mission statement should say something about your desire for marriage. Want to be a parent? Your mission statement and life experience should say something about your abilities as a parent.

> *...we glory in tribulations also: knowing that tribulation worketh patience; And patience, experience; and experience, hope* (Romans 5:3-4).

So we see from this verse that when you are able to overcome tribulation or hardness, you perfect endurance and that endurance gives you the experience which in turn produces hope. Your resume should describe your ability to endure, the patience you perfected, and the hope others can glean that you will be able to repeat this success. I have provided a vague sample of my own Emotional Resume to be a mom. Although I didn't have the savvy title I am offering you today, I did frame my own personal argument to convince myself of my parental competency.

## EVELYN D. WATKINS

### *Objectives*

To be a Godly mother whose children call blessed (Prov. 31:28)

### *Mission*

To create children who know they are loved, wanted, celebrated, and cherished who realize their God-given potential and fulfill their divine purpose.

### *Education*

- ♥ Early Childhood Education
- ♥ *Parenting is not for Cowards*
- ♥ *What to Expect in the Early Years*
- ♥ *Mothers and Daughters in the Adolescent Years*

♥ Attended Multiple Marriage and
Family Conferences

### Experience

♥ Aunt & Caregiver 1983 – Present

♥ God Mother 1993 – Present

I was responsible for providing a safe environment for children to visit. I trained to provide pediatric CPR and first aid and also studied parenting basics. Learned the appropriate foods, snacks, and equipment suitable for both young and older children. Had to plan activities and meals for nieces each summer during their annual trip away from their parents. Assured that I knew the relevant educational toys, games, and television programs for children. Provided care in a thoughtful, compassionate, and temperate manner.

### Skills

Creative and dramatic reader. Innovative player who can create games with little or no resources. Silly and fun loving. Extremely temperate and patient. High energy and endurance. Can perform cartwheels, tumbles, splits, and flips. Can improvise to create songs and stories as well as develop my own dance recital in the kitchen. Take great pictures and am a natural exhorter. Identifies the gifts of others easily.

Love to hug, smooch, and tickle. Possess at least seventy-five terms of endearment that all children love. Affirming, gentle, reassuring, and protective. Can throw a fantastic pink pajama party, miniature tea party, or Talent Show. Can cover and exhort through trayer.

### References

G. Cox, A. Thomas, A. Kearse, C. Dobbs, D. Nargassans

CHAPTER SEVEN

# FORGIVENESS: THE POWER TO SAVE YOURSELF

This is the turning point of breaking up the stony ground of our heart; it's called forgiveness. There are many great books and reference guides on the topic, but I choose to hone in on the biblical facets of forgiveness because they are quite illuminating and the evidence of its effectiveness transcends all creeds. Forgiveness not only releases the burden of debt placed on your offender, but it frees you to receive forgiveness and opens the hidden spaces of your heart to receive love.

Let's examine first the process of forgiveness. Forgiveness is a choice. We can't say, "I can't forgive them," because actually you can. Forgiveness is an act of your will. You can choose to do it. If you want to break away the callousness of your heart, forgiveness must be a part of the process.

I remember reflecting this concept and thinking, "I don't want to have to ask the men who molested me to apologize." Well, I didn't. I didn't need to ask them to apologize to extend forgiveness. This is a tough concept for many because some of us are waiting for people to come to the revelation that they've hurt us. We're waiting for the apology.

Unfortunately, they may never come to that revelation; meanwhile, we are in desperate need of an open heart. So the need to forgive is something we are compelled to do for our emotional well-being.

Forgiveness says I GIVE mercy FOR nothing. Mercy is given, not because someone deserves it but because we are made like our God; merciful.

Here is the first benefit of forgiveness:

> *For if you forgive people their trespasses [their reck-*
> *less and willful sins, leaving them, letting them go,*
> *and giving up resentment], your heavenly Father*
> *will also forgive you* (Matthew 6:14 AMP).

I love the way the Amplified Bible states it: *leaving them, letting them go, and giving up resentment.* How beautiful. It is a giving up. A surrender of the will. So when you give up and surrender and say, "I choose not to be resentful toward you," you can actively experience the power of extending forgiveness.

Have you ever played tag with friends and you were caught up in the activity of someone chasing you and chasing you. You were winded, exhausted, and out of breath. Your lungs burned and legs ached and then finally you said, "I give...I give...I give up!" Do you remember how that felt? Exhilaration. Relief. Rest. That's what forgiveness feels like. It's as though resentment, bitterness, anger, and sorrow are chasing you and you finally say, "I give up." It is freedom.

Now you may choose to tell the person who has hurt you that you forgive them. This may or may not be advisable. Consider who you will be talking to. Consider if perhaps an argument or further division will take place as a result of this action. Again, you are doing this to free yourself and not necessarily to reignite a new relationship with your offender.

*Confess your faults one to another, and pray one for another, that ye may be healed. The effectual fervent prayer of a righteous man availeth much* (James 5:16).

The above verse speaks to sharing your faults with one another and praying. This is an important part of the puzzle. You may be saying, "well they hurt me; what is my fault in this?" The answer: holding the unforgiveness, holding onto the offense, and allowing it to hinder you from loving the way you should.

It also says that you tell others (i.e. a friend, confidante, counselor, or therapist) of your challenge for the purpose of YOUR healing. This process has nothing to do with them and everything to do with you. Let's say for example, you tell your offender (if it is ideal) "I have had ought against you and I would like for you to forgive me for the ought. Furthermore, I want you to know that I forgive you for the offense." Now you may need to let a good friend know that you have done this and ask them to pray for you. Pray that you are able to now walk in forgiveness; not just talking about it with your lips but able to walk it out.

In sharing it with someone else, you have now employed a form of accountability. You will not be able to talk about that issue with this person again without them correcting you for your contrary behavior. You will not be able to treat a new man in your life as though he is completely untrustworthy based on the actions of an unfaithful ex-husband. This accountability friend won't allow it.

So go ahead and forgive that person today. I'm going to ask you to write a letter of forgiveness to that person. Included in your letter, should be the power or benefit you expect to obtain as a result of forgiving that person.

For example, when I had to really overcome resentment toward my foster mother for not protecting me from her boyfriend's advances, I had to write: *"I forgive you for your failure to protect me. Your unwillingness to stand up for me and protect me is probably a result of no one protecting you as a young girl. For that, I am sorry for you. I forgive you for creating an environment which was so frightening, I feared sleeping at night. Because I have forgiven you, I possess the power to protect my girls. I am sensitive to know all truth concerning them and I have communicated uncompromising commitment to protect them from anyone who would attempt to do them harm. I am a better discerner of evil because of this experience and have placed it in its proper place in my life. You are forgiven."*

People often ask, "How will I know when I really have forgiven someone?" Well, you will have forgiven them when you say you have forgiven them. It is done by faith. You will know with certainty that your forgiveness is durable when your thoughts concerning that person have changed. When you ponder their name and a different, perhaps merciful image takes residence in your eyes.

For example, if every time someone mentions your ex-husband's name, you roll your eyes and think of the woman he left you for, you're probably still in the active forgiveness stage. If you see a former co-worker on the street and you think of how she sabotaged you and cost you your job, you're probably still in the active forgiveness stage. It's a process and with time, your first thought will not be the event but perhaps the children, job, or need for healing associated with that person.

I'm sure you've heard people say, "I forgive you but I sure won't forget what you did!" Well you don't suddenly get amnesia, however, there should be a part of you that does forget with time.

Let's examine Hebrews 10:17 (KJV):

*And their sins and iniquities will I remember no more.*

Of course we know God is God. Of course He knows and remembers. What the verse tells us is that He doesn't hold us hostage to our faults. He doesn't look at us and see our shortcomings.

This is how I packaged the pair: forgiveness is for giving and forgetting is for getting. Forgiveness gives you the opportunity to get what you thought you had to give away. My forgiving an old friend for gossiping about me and choosing to forget the occurrence when I see her avails me the opportunity to *get* a stronger friendship with someone who will *give* me loyalty.

Remember how I shared with you the power of the written word? Writing it down is so very powerful. When the feeling begins to well up in you in the future, you can say as Jesus did. Simply say, "it is written...," and quote whatever you wrote in your forgiveness letter.

Begin to ponder on the benefits of your giving mercy to others. Imagine how your life will be different as a result of being able to look others in the eye without any disdain. Try to imagine how you will be able to teach other women or your children the importance and power of forgiveness and what it gives you.

With that in mind, list explicitly what giving mercy to others gives you. More importantly, write down how you imagine your relationships with others may be enhanced through this process.

I remember being a guarded person who would never allow myself to be vulnerable with other women. I had perfected the act of being able to share very intimate things all while being emotionally cut off from the experience. In doing so, the hearers thought I was having a tender moment with them, when in fact I had no feeling in sharing these deep stories or experiences. It was as though it had happened to someone else. I compartmentalized the entire experience.

It wasn't until I could really visualize my pain and go through the process of true forgiveness did I then feel moved by my own words. Before your words move others, they should first move you. Do they?

CHAPTER EIGHT

# FINDING AN EXAMPLE

I can't remember what the weather was that day. What I was wearing. Or how I arrived. In fact, I can't even remember why that eleven-year-old girl strolled into McDonald's that day. I simply recall being third in line. A man stood at the counter giving his order, making small talk with the cashier. In front of me stood a woman who today I simply refer to as the "*woman in red*." She was striking to me. Her petite frame seemed perfect to me in every way. Slender and poised in her tailored red suit. Her jacket landed just below her buttocks and her skirt just above her knee. She wore sheer white stockings with three-inch high heels. Her blonde hair swooped the nape of her neck then danced across her shoulders as if orchestrated to do so. Her wrists were so tiny, the watch on her left hand dangled a bit. Her nails were carefully painted red as though intentionally planned to match her outfit. And, oh my, what a wedding ring. I imagined what her life must be like. Her husband...did she have children? I guessed she had to be the best kind of mother there was. Had to be. Her husband probably greeted her with a kiss each night when he came home.

She had the aroma of wealth. Her fragrance, so distinct, seemed to tickle my nose. Surely this is what rich people smelled like. She turned her head gently to the right and I saw her face. She was as beautiful as I imagined. Her skin was like milky white porcelain. How could lips be so red? Or cheeks so gently stained pink? She was simply exquisite. Impeccable. Divine. In that moment, I knew I wanted to be just like her.

Her poise, grace, beauty, and infectious scent. "May I help you?" the cashier asked. The object of my attention seemed to glide to the cashier. "Coffee, regular." Just those two words. Nothing else. She looked back at me, as though checking on me and simply grinned without showing her teeth. She exuded such genuine warmth. "I want that," I thought.

As an overweight child, I didn't think I could have her slender, petite frame. As a black girl, I thought for sure the blonde hair thing was out and the milky white skin was a definite impossibility. My hands, even at just eleven, seemed more like a lumberjacks than the dainty ring-holders she sported. As a foster child, I knew I was too poor to smell that rich. But as she pivoted and walked away, I knew with certainty that I could glean something to be like this remarkable *woman in red*.

"May I help you?" the cashier inquired, breaking my gaze from my oblivious mentor. Just then I realized I had completely forgotten what I was supposed to purchase. As though by instinct, I clamored, "Coffee, regular." The cashier quickly took my one-dollar bill and handed me three silver coins. "One moment, please," she stammered as she quickly poured the coffee. "Have a good day," she concluded. "Thank you," I replied, beaming at the thought of having something exactly the same as my *woman in red*. I gently picked it up and attempted to arrange my fingers as she had around the hot cup. I, too, pivoted and walked out. I'm sure I fumbled out as I had on my way in but in my mind I was floating across the floor. I wanted so desperately to be her; but if not, I could at least have what she was having "coffee, regular." From that day to this, I am slightly hypnotized by the smell of coffee. I have had periods in my life where I consumed upwards of twelve cups a day. Imagine, an obsession initiated by a perfect stranger. She became my standard for the total package. I didn't have any real-life women in my life at that time who met that visual standard, but over thirty years later her presence is as clear as it was that memorable day in McDonald's.

Problem is, when you are trying to find a model for internal change, looking at a distant unknown example is oftentimes deceiving. I can't tell you the number of people who are stunned when they discover that someone they really admire isn't quite all they thought they were. Parishioners who discover that their pastor doesn't pray day and night or that he and his wife do not pray together each morning. The celebrity with the great body has a great airbrushed body. That great married couple isn't so great behind closed doors. The problem with modeling people you don't know is that you really don't know them! So you are attempting to model an ideal rather than a real person. So my lady in red was and still is my visual model, but for me to know how to be a loving person, friend, mom, wife, and leader, I would need to have real models, real mentors in my life who could help me slough away my rough edges.

In my lifetime, I have had a few women who have made significant impact in my life. I didn't have just one and you may not be able to find just one who possesses the qualities you need. Because I moved so often as a young girl and was never nurtured as a young woman, I was very needy in many, many ways and thus needed guidance on diverse fronts.

I'm going to share with you the first woman I met who began my evolution into the woman in red. I took a summer job with the Neighborhood Youth Corp (NYC) during my junior/senior years of high school. The organization placed at-risk inner city kids and wards of the state with employers who would expose them to a progressive and professional work environment. The hope was that the young people would learn from their full-time employer and perhaps be inspired to make wise choices for their future and learn some new skills along the way. Well, this would be my second employer with NYC and my assignment was with Massachusetts Public Defenders. They were the complimentary criminal trial attorneys for accused felons who could not afford their own attorney. The manager of this important office was Dianne. The first day at the office I was greeted by this strikingly tall woman at 5'11" (I'm 5'3"). She had brown shoulder-length hair, blue-green eyes, and the biggest smile I ever saw. And did I mention she had on a red suit? She greeted me with a warm hello and was a bit impressed that I was dressed professionally and arrived on time. Seems my predecessors didn't take this opportunity so seriously. Dianne was engaged to one of the attorneys in the firm and sported the largest diamond ring I ever saw. She and I hit it off immediately. We discovered that we both were raised on Chandler Street (when I lived with my own mother) and yearned for a better future. She was in the midst of planning for her big wedding which would happen the following year and I was smack dab in the middle of all of that excitement.

Dianne took me under her wing. She brought me to her new home she and her fiancé bought and joined me for lunch frequently. I observed her respect for those she worked with; I witnessed the mercy she had on me and I relished in the many invitations to parties—she seemed to leap at the opportunity to include me. I was just seventeen years old and she was thirty. I never felt in the way, irrelevant, or unprotected. She looked out for me and allowed me to peer into her life to see what was possible for me. What if I could buy a home with an atrium and a hot tub in the middle of the house? What if I could marry someone so important and command the respect of my peers? What if I could be a mom who was so patient, tender, and kind? Dianne's role in my life began as a witness to what was possible.

The most impressive female mentoring relationship I've found is actually in the Bible and is that of Naomi and Ruth. After the death of her husband and brother-in-law at war, Ruth commits to follow Naomi, her mother-in-law. Naomi attempts to discourage Ruth to no avail. A lot of times, people who you desire to mentor you may discourage you from doing so. I know I've done that to other women. Perhaps I didn't think I was quite the example they needed or more importantly, I didn't have the time to invest in the kind of guidance they needed.

Well Ruth persists, and declares that she will make Naomi's God her God and Naomi's people will be her people.

## 1. Be sure when seeking a mentor/model that you are following people of like faith.

> *And Ruth said, Intreat me not to leave thee, or to return from following after thee: for whither thou goest, I will go; and where thou lodgest, I will lodge: thy people shall be my people, and thy God my God* (Ruth 1:16).

I made a major move from Massachusetts to Georgia. Before, during, and after I consulted with my oldest sister April. She and her husband Charles were pastors in Massachusetts. They were concerned not only about my ability to remain economically stable and thriving, they also were keenly concerned about my spiritual connection and growth. As such, my sister would consistently hold me accountable to a respectable lifestyle. When I told them I had found a church, they requested tapes of the sermons, notes from the New Members classes, and soon took a trip to Atlanta to visit the church firsthand and assure it was suitable. They were pleased with my choice and remained involved supporters and advisors to my spiritual growth. This lady in red was both my genetic and spiritual sister and I was quite grateful to have her.

## 2. Your mentor should have visible increase in her life.

> So Naomi returned, and Ruth the Moabitess,
> her daughter in law, with her,...and they came
> to Bethlehem in the beginning of barley harvest
> (Ruth 1:22).

When Ruth followed Naomi, they showed up in Bethlehem at the beginning of harvest. If your mentor is going to teach you anything, she has to at least be at the beginning of increase or success from her own journey. In other words, if you're trying to stop drinking alcohol and you are looking for someone to encourage you along the way it should be someone who has at least begun the journey and had a positive harvest or success. Weight loss tips are best harnessed from someone who has actually lost weight. Parenting tips are best attained from women who actually have children, not just read about them. When I met my friend Dianne, she was just beginning a whole new life which held lots of tangibles I desired. She was a perfect mentor for me to visibly witness that which I would eventually desire to glean.

## 3. Your mentor should possess the influence to allow you to abide and/or work in places you don't necessarily belong.

> Then said Boaz unto Ruth, Hearest thou not,
> my daughter? Go not to glean in another field,
> neither go from hence, but abide here fast by my

*maidens: Let thine eyes be on the field that they
do reap, and go thou after them* (Ruth 2:8-9).

Boaz allowed Ruth to work in the field where his maidens worked. She was elevated in position to be able to work alongside his maidens. I remember Dianne making sure I was invited to a Bar Association party when our head attorney received a judgeship. It was remarkable that I was there, that she endorsed me and made others believe I belonged there. There were many other times when she opened doors to allow me to be present in places I didn't belong or hadn't earned the right to abide.

### 4. *Your mentor should provide you with protection.*

*Have I not charged the young men that they shall
not touch thee?* (Ruth 2:9)

The Amplified Bible says, *"Have I not charged the young men not to molest you?"* I'm sure you can imagine that this was a big passage for me. Your mentor should be able to cover you and protect you. She should be able to see things you can't see. Those who molest girls and boys are often defined as monsters but that title blurs their personhood. These assailants are merely your neighbors, teachers, doctors, and church members. A seasoned mentor will have the ability to discern those who would desire to hurt you. The hurt doesn't have to be the result of sexual robbery, it can be financial manipulation or emotional theft.

I met a strong mentor in Georgia. She is twelve years my senior and had a wealth of knowledge. She was truly a virtuous woman in every sense of the word and I learned much from her. Her greatest asset to me during those early days was her discernment and boldness. She, being much more mature and seasoned than I, was able to sense if a friendship was toxic or could be fruitful. She would tell me what she witnessed and how I should practically manage the matter. She was very wise and unafraid to rebuke the young men whose intentions were not pure. She would call me late in the evening to make sure I was home and to make sure there wasn't anyone there with me. She was instrumental in guarding my celibacy; she was a good godly covering and assured that I was never "touched."

5. *Your mentor should be willing to share their reward.*

> *...and when thou art athirst, go unto the vessels, and drink of that which the young men have drawn* (Ruth 2:9).

Boaz charged Ruth to drink the water that his workers had already drawn. He essentially said you may have what you haven't labored for. Your mentor should want to extend to you their insight, secrets, expertise, and substance; even if you didn't work for it.

My friend Betty has proven to be an irreplaceable asset as a mom. To me, she is the quintessential mother. Patient, kind, smart, challenging, involved, committed, and very learned. Betty's daughter Dina is six years older than my oldest daughter so I have the continued benefit of learning from what she has already done. She is extremely honest about her successes and shortcomings. She also is committed to send me everything and I do mean everything that was ever written about being a great mom. She photocopies articles, copies pages from books, and forwards her own daughter's writings. If I suggest that the information she sent was helpful, the entire book shows up a week later. Her insight, experience, and research is truly a gift which is not easily replaced.

### 6.  *Your mentor's relationships will extend favor to you.*

> *Then she fell on her face, and bowed herself to the ground, and said unto him, Why have I found grace in thine eyes, that thou shouldest take knowledge of me, seeing I am a stranger?*
>
> *And Boaz answered and said unto her, It hath fully been shewed me, all that thou hast done unto thy mother in law since the death of thine husband* (Ruth 2:10-11).

Ruth's relationship with her mother-in-law opened the door of favor in her life. This can be a trickier relationship to find but it is possible. I extend favor to women around me all the time. They get opportunities they have not earned, go places they do not pay for, and receive jobs they may not have been experienced enough to obtain on their own. But it is my pleasure to extend my favorable relationship with them so they can progress in ways that they may not have otherwise.

Take the time to ponder these points. Again, it may not be possible to find one person who encompasses all of these qualities, but perhaps there are several who meet the criteria. When I was concerned that I would be verbally or physically abusive, it became necessary for me to pay attention to people like Dianne and Betty who demonstrated the tenderness I naturally lacked. They treated their daughters with dignity and respect which I was uncertain I had the capacity to do. When I wasn't sure I could be a supportive wife, I looked to my sister April, who made temperance and honor look as easy as breathing. I'll never measure up to her example but she has demonstrated that women like me, with our unique background, can be teachable, supportive, and loving.

CHAPTER NINE

KNOWING YOU

When we endure the process of tearing away at hardness, the challenge can be our ability to recognize our own self. I had experienced a time in my life when I had become so enthralled with being this covered-up phony, that when it came time to tear away to the core of who I was, I was confused about me. Who was I...really? It was a scary process, because once you tear down the walls of who you believed "you" were, you may find that you are left with a woman who may be much more docile, sensitive, feminine, and vulnerable than anything you ever imagined.

Once free, you may find yourself to be one who tells people immediately how you feel: you're beautiful, I love you, I appreciate you, or you hurt me. This may look a bit daunting, but it is the way we were made. We were made to speak out of the fullness of our heart. Many of us have trained ourselves to not speak at all, to not make waves. Others are good at speaking the rough stuff; you know, getting people told off. But many of us suffer at sharing out of the beauty of our heart. The Bible tells us that the heart and the mouth are connected and the mouth is created to be a reflection of a full heart.

> *...out of the abundance of the heart the mouth speaketh* (Matthew 12:34).

So here we see that the fullness of the heart should cause our mouth to speak in kind. As you notice your words changing, you can rejoice in knowing that your heart is changing.

But who is the new you? Be assured that we do know our self, in spite of what magazines or talk shows may say. We do know who we are. It may be a little fuzzy, particularly after we have purged our heart.

> *For what person perceives (knows and understands) what passes through a man's thoughts except the man's own spirit within him? Just so no one discerns (comes to know and comprehend) the thoughts of God except the Spirit of God* (1 Corinthians 2:11 AMP).

As you can see, no one knows you like you know you. Therefore, take the time to acknowledge this new woman you are evolving into. Don't allow your past to continue to define who you are and your possibilities.

I remember after years of struggling with my weight, I had lost about sixty pounds. For the first time as a woman, I had a very lean body. I can recall being in a dressing room at a store called Tempo Fashions. I reached for my usual size 15/16, and the pants dropped to the floor. Keep in mind, I didn't lose the weight in a week, yet I was astonished that these pants did not fit. I continued trying on clothes; one size after the other until I held a size 3/4 and to my shock, it fit.

I remember turning around and around and wondering how this happened. It was truly an epiphany. I could not see my body as it was because I was so accustomed to seeing myself fat. So although my facts had changed, the truth I lived with each day had not enlightened my own eyes.

It took a period of time to see myself as I was. Changed. Some of us are not quite so good about seeing our reality and need outside assistance. So what I would recommend is that you ask someone else, who they believe you are, and what people in general believe concerning you. Look at what Jesus asked of the disciples.

> *And He said to them, But who do you [yourselves] say that I am? And Peter replied, The Christ of God!* (Luke 9:20 AMP)

You notice Jesus is interested in what His disciples thought of Him. Oftentimes, we may feel a bit arrogant and think, "I don't care what people think." Well, Jesus cared. We don't concern ourselves for the purposes of bondage, but we should care. Knowing what others think can be pretty telling as to who we are. It is not necessarily our truth, but nonetheless, it tells us a great deal as to how the world perceives us. Remember, like me, many of you may think you are hiding something. But again, like me, the only one deceived may be you. Ask people you trust who they believe you are and examine the contrast with what you know of yourself.

There are those who will help you to see your growth, your progress, and evolution into the woman whose heart is pliable, loveable, and ready to love others.

I would encourage you to complete a self-describing task. Write a biography of your life. It should be limited to your personal experiences and not professional achievements. It's not a book, just a snapshot of your experiences. The painful ones and the ones worthy of rejoicing. It should come to an end with your today. Your purging, forgiveness, and the new woman who has been birthed as a result.

# CHAPTER TEN

# GOD'S GRACE

Just as we mentioned that the body attempts to heal itself, God too sends us relationships that are designed to be a prescription for health. I call them grace relationships.

Despite my many tumultuous stories, I have had my share of grace relationships too. They have been like a small scalpel, scraping away at the calcification bit by bit. In the next chapter we will discuss what actions you have to take; but here, we are talking about what God gives or more plainly, who he sends.

Grace relationships do not wipe the slate clean, they simply give you the courage to pick up the cloth and cleanser to do the work yourself.

You heard the story of my fourth grade teacher who underscored a continuing theme in my life, "unforgettable." Well, I had a third grade teacher named Mrs. Mary Sullivan. She was indeed a grace relationship. She secretly invited me and another student (he had twelve siblings) to her home a few weeks before Christmas.

She lived in a suburb outside of the city and it was probably the first time I had seen the countryside. We accompanied her to a hockey game for her son then back to her house and to see some horses in the neighborhood. We played with her children for hours. After dinner, she invited us down the steps to her finished basement den. There sat a beautifully decorated Christmas tree with a slew of gifts festively wrapped underneath. To our surprise, the nearly twenty-five presents under the tree were for me and my classmate. I was stunned.

I think on some level I realized she may have felt bad for us. Nevertheless, there were many occasions for people to be sympathetic and do something extraordinary, but they didn't. Her grace relationship message: you are worth sacrifice, advance planning, and celebration.

In sixth grade, Miss Carol Perry took her entire class under her wings. St. Nicholas Elementary was nestled in a high-risk neighborhood. My sixth grade there was one of the best and most memorable years of school. Miss Perry was a Christian and managed to slide religious tracts, paraphernalia, and songs into her sixth-grade class. She was an outstanding giver who touched each child in the class in a very real way. She was big on hugs and big on love. Her grace relationship: you can be hugged and held in a pure way.

My friend Dianne was also a grace relationship. At age seventeen, I told Dianne that I had never had a birthday party. Seemed like at the office they were always having cakes and celebrations for one reason or another. In a light-hearted casual conversation, I explained to her how Mrs. Adamitis had forgotten my cupcake and Golden Book. The following summer when I went to work there, Dianne planned an office party for me. It was the most beautiful cake I had ever seen and the conference room was adorned with balloons. She bought me flowers and a wonderful book. I was taken aback at the fact that she remembered my little story from the year before; that it moved her and provoked her to remember me a whole year later. Years later, Dianne would remember my daughter's birthdays, Easter, Valentine's Day, and Christmas each year with a gift, a card, and sometimes a little cash inside just like a grandmother would. My girls know well that their Auntie Dianne always remembers them. This grace relationship taught me: you are remembered. You are noticed and you are not forgotten.

> *But not as the offense, so also is the free gift. For if through the offense of one many be dead, much more the grace of God, and the gift by grace, which is by one man, Jesus Christ, hath abounded unto many* (Romans 5:15).

I love the concept of grace: it freely overtakes the offense which would bring about death and allows life to spring forward.

My grace relationships were freely offered, most of them for just a season. Their object was to overtake an offense and allow life to spring forward. Can you recount relationships in your life which you know were specifically assigned to you, destined by God for the purpose of bringing more life to your life? In John 10:10 it says, *"I am come that they might have life, and that they might have it more abundantly."*

Take a moment and list the grace relationships you have encountered and describe how they have added more life to your life.

## CHAPTER ELEVEN

# TAKE ACTION

I am hopeful that you are ready to put more action to this process. The process of faith requires action.

> *Are you willing to be shown [proof], ...that faith apart from [good] works is inactive and ineffective and worthless?* (James 2:20 AMP)

So without the works, our faith is ineffective or worthless. So let's put our faith to work. Let me give you the easiest way for you to change your heart. It's called seed time. You cannot produce a behavior and not receive a harvest of the same behavior. If you extend forgiveness, you will reap forgiveness. If you extend love, you will reap love. The Bible says if a man desires a friend, let him show himself friendly.

> *Be not deceived; God is not mocked: for whatsoever a man soweth, that shall he also reap* (Galatians 6:7).

This teaches us that you will absolutely receive a harvest off of your seed. It is a guarantee as certain as gravity. Doesn't matter if you believe it or not. If you are kind, you will get kindness back. So you have to begin to look at your life now and assess whether or not you are dwelling in the kind of harvest life you desire.

I recall being very concerned about the kind of mother I would be someday because of the treatment I received as a child. I feared I was destined to be an abuser. My response to that was to find children with whom I could sow kindness and love. Find children whom I could give gifts to and hug, adorn with kisses in a holy manner. In doing this, I healed my own brokenness, created a new characteristic to my personality, and redirected my destiny.

I have done similar behaviors with women. Where I lacked mentors, and resented women who neglected or refused to invest in my training, I in turn found other women whom I could impart, train, and mentor. In doing so, I healed my own brokenness, added a new character trait (exhorter), and redirected my destiny.

This was the key to the battle with my weight. Acknowledge the pain, forgive the molester, become one who encouraged others through their pain, and thus create a new destiny for my body.

You must find someone or many whom you can sow the results you desire. You have to deliberately, on purpose, tell others you love them, if this is an area where you were neglected. You have to find children to love, if this is an area where you need healing. You must find a wife to befriend and encourage, if that was something you desperately needed during your difficult marriage. Rescue one who is abused. Do whatever it takes to sow what you wish you received.

Back in high school when I began my first part-time job, I used my paycheck to lavish friends and family with gifts. I didn't realize at the time that I was sowing what I desired but that is exactly what I was doing. And it felt great.

My first friend in high school, Iris, was the recipient of a luxurious rabbit coat with matching gloves. I took great care to assure the box was beautifully wrapped and complemented the extravagance of the gift inside. She received my token of affection with exuberant joy. It was exactly what I had hoped for. Iris was my friend, the first at this new school, North High. She was a beautiful Puerto Rican girl whose substance in life was probably as meager as my own. For this reason, gifting her was a terrific pleasure. I gave to her the way I had always wanted to receive from others and it was more than satisfying...it was healing.

I learned many biblical principles during my young life, absent of Sunday school, regular church attendance, or spiritual parenting. My lessons at the time were instinctual. My giving to Iris illuminated the Bible verse to do unto others as you would have them do unto you.

> *And as ye would that men should do to you, do ye also to them likewise* (Luke 6:31).

No one had taught me that principle just yet, but life had demonstrated the rich reward of sowing your desires into others. Its reward could not be contained in a package but was able to flood the empty depths of my heart, filling it with the love I deeply yearned to receive.

There are countless books written on the process, importance, and power of giving. Giving in this fashion should not be confused with merely the Christian laws of giving and receiving. The return on your giving in this measure should be a soulish or emotional gain, not necessarily tangible in nature.

I spent many years hearing the church offering messages stating to "give and it shall be given."

> *Give and it shall be given unto you, good measure, pressed down, and shaken together, and running over, shall men give into your bosom. For with the same measure that ye mete withal it shall be measured to you again* (Luke 6:38).

When placing money in the offering plate, many ponder this in hopes of seeing the return of the check they just dropped, only with perhaps a little interest added on top. If this idea of giving is what you embrace in this process, you will probably be slightly disappointed.

Tangible things are not going to repair a hardened heart. That Golden Book and Hostess Cupcake was cheap in terms of its monetary value, but weighty in its ability to prove that *I had value.*

## GIVE WHILE IT HURTS

When my husband and I decided to begin a family we quickly discovered that birth control really didn't control birth at all. As a young couple, we never imagined that it would be difficult to conceive. After five years of ovulation studies, surgery, and specimen handling, Dr. Cabrera solemnly explained that we were not good candidates for in vitro and pregnancy would probably not be a reality for us.

To add to my disappointment, it seemed that my friends who had married around the same time as me were now pregnant and on this new journey of expectation. I had to rejoice for them, although it was very difficult, I knew with certainty it was what God expected of me.

> *Rejoice with them that do rejoice, and weep with them that weep* (Romans 12:15).

Remember I wrote about the ability to be moved, or touched by people? Having empathy and a depth of compassion for the experiences of others is not limited simply to the hardships of people but the celebratory moments as well.

I honestly believe that from the second year of our pregnancy attempts until the third, someone I loved was pregnant. I had to revert back to: *And as ye would that men should do to you, do ye also to them likewise.* And doing likewise isn't just "kinda rejoicing." It's a full-throttle, over-the-top, "I am thrilled for you!" and what I am giving or doing is going to reflect that emotion.

I gave "over-the-top" baby showers, with "over-the-top" gifts, and cooked "over-the-top" meals for my morning-sick friends. As I blessed each person throughout their pregnancy, I became more at peace with my childlessness and my ever-increasing role as godmother to many. The sadness and sorrow from my barrenness was replaced with the joy of being able (time, energy, and finances) to be helpful to these new moms and be a blessing to their children.

They were receiving lots of support and tangible things from me, but honestly, I was the richer for the opportunity to give of myself and substance. What I needed in this instance wasn't baby things, but the intangible residue to fill the empty place in my heart where my desire to be a mother was positioned. The inadequacy was replaced by a sense of necessity. I was needed by these women: to encourage them, tell them they were doing a great job, relieve them so they could have a well-needed break. The place in my heart that questioned "what if I am not a reproductive being" was replaced by this emerging destiny of exhorter and mentor. I was complete.

I don't want to imply that giving does not replicate after its kind, because it does. I am merely suggesting that when your objective is to become whole, the return on investment you seek should come in the form of emotional revenue rather than any physical asset.

One of the baby showers I gave during my season of barrenness went to a woman who was newly married, living in an apartment which was just large enough for herself, her husband, and her child from a previous relationship. When I discovered she was pregnant, I felt a little sad, because I knew she would not have significant resources to have the nursery and all of the hoopla we like to have when preparing for a new baby in a new marriage. I had just gotten laid off from my job, but made a commitment to her. I told her to find a crib and changing table that she wanted and I would buy it for her. I told her not to choose anything cheap, just find what she wanted and it would be my pleasure to give it to her. I prayed and asked God to bless me to be a blessing to her. I really wanted to be the one to purchase her nursery furniture. I needed a job, and not surprisingly, God's faithfulness persevered. I gave her the money for her nursery and months later hosted a baby shower for her.

Five years later, she and many others who knew of my plight in becoming pregnant received a custom announcement in the mail.

> In a few months we'll need a new carriage
>
> To hold our new baby, God's gift to our marriage
>
> We wanted to share our exciting news with you
>
> And request your prayers for us and baby Watkins, too!

A little over-the-top, right? But remember, that's what I was accustomed to doing by now. People who I hardly knew rejoiced. Church members who saw my husband and I walk to the altar for prayer for infertility rejoiced. And of course, friends rejoiced.

From the moment of the announcement, I received gifts from all over the country. Old friends, family members, and colleagues sent well wishes, prayers, and notes to build my confidence. Several women took over the planning of my baby shower and it was produced with great excellence. There were maybe sixty people there, and the menu was exceptional. It was exactly what I would have done for myself...perhaps better. My sister April flew in from Massachusetts. And it truly was an over-the-top harvest, received from much sowing of the same.

There was something missing. The woman whom I purchased the nursery furniture for, the one whom I prayed to God for so that he would give me a job so I could bless her, the one whom I also hosted a baby shower for, didn't come. She didn't call. She didn't send her regrets, nothing. She didn't send flowers or a card when the baby was born. Nothing. But my giving to her was about *her receiving tangible things*; not me. It was about her feeling celebrated; not me. I had already received my reward. A fullness in a barren heart. I did not need her to reciprocate. I would be lying if I said her absence went unnoticed. I was puzzled at the thoughtlessness of it all, however, I didn't need her gift. I actually didn't need her celebration either. I had an abundance of both already. If no one had hosted a shower or expressed how happy they were for me, I would have still had plenty of "stuff," and more importantly, I stored rejoicing in my own heart for such a time as this.

On the side of the driveway of a home we custom built were several medium-size boulders which direct water down the slope. We moved into the house in January and were quite surprised that summer when we saw a watermelon growing through the rocks. We built this house ourselves, we knew what was on the property, and we directed the landscapers and nowhere was watermelon part of our exterior plan. It was no small watermelon. It was huge. We marveled at it and wondered if someone just threw watermelon out there somewhere and the seeds took root or if something airborne had planted it there. Either way, no one was expecting a watermelon harvest there, in rocks on the side of the slope.

We lived in that home for thirteen years and never had another watermelon grow there or anywhere on our property again. Just that one time.

What that watermelon underscores is that when you cast seed, you will receive a harvest. End of story. The seed will bring fruit of its kind with certainty. The fruit, however, may not necessarily come up where it was originally planted. When the wind blows, seeds are carried to different places. Bees help carry seed to different places. Raking your yard can inadvertently carry seeds to places you didn't expect. This is important because as I mentioned earlier when discussing forgiveness, you may not get what you want from the person you want it. You may not get an apology from the actual person who harmed you. You may not get recognition from the person who you helped to promote. And you may not receive a gift from the person you gifted. This is why you have to examine what form of return you want on your investment. I know for me, I am in search of the intangible return, knowing that the tangible gift is guaranteed.

God will never be mocked. Whatever you sow you shall surely reap. This is not a punishment Scripture, but a covenant promise.

> *Be not deceived; God is not mocked: for whatsoever a man soweth, that shall he also reap* (Galatians 6:7).

CHAPTER TWELVE

# YOUR NEW HEART

Have you ever observed a young child, say four or five, who has a very active rough and tumble life? Have you ever noticed that with all the bumps, bruises, and even breaks, their scars heal quickly and they seem to be right back in the game of doing all the daring things that caused their injuries in the beginning? This is the analogy I like to use concerning recognizing the finished work. I started this book with the analogy of the foot, the hardened skin, and its useless ugliness. Once you see a good podiatrist (if necessary) or obtain a great pedicure, you can sport sandals without anyone ever knowing that you once had hard dead skin at the bottom of your sole.

My hope is that at the end of your process, when you are stripped down, no one will ever know what you had at the bottom of your soul!

That little five-year-old, like my Noelle, who proudly wears her Band-Aid, has too much living to do to be afraid to jump off the sofa again. She loves life too much to be concerned with avoiding the ramp on the driveway which I tell her again and again is much too dangerous for her Princess bicycle. The beauty of her reckless curiosity is that when she does fall, and gets her new bandage, just days later she can't tell you where exactly her "boo boo" is. It simply is no longer visible. She can remember the courageous, high-flying ride which ended in a knee-skinning spill, but she can't find the scar on her body. No evidence of a scar and no fear to engage in life again, open to the possibility of being hurt and yet pursuing it anyway. This is my desire for you. It is God's desire for us all.

> *And be renewed in the spirit of your mind* (Ephesians 4:23).

I am renewed. A new person, inside and out, because I have renewed the spirit of my mind. I've committed to renew my soul, my thoughts, my emotions, and engage in life unafraid of the possibility of hurt.

When I am out speaking, oftentimes I'll share a story of the power to overcome and will without thought share a story like one in this book or one of countless others. At the end of my conference or seminar, someone will undoubtedly approach me and say, "I would have never believed you were obese...or abused...or insecure, you seem so confident and self-assured. Wow." And I tell them as I will tell you now; that is what wholeness looks like. I'm not in denial that there was pain or even brokenness for that matter. I simply no longer have the scars. The evidence of their existence is gone. When women look at me now, they see the "woman in red." A woman whom others want to mimic, who yearn to know her more, who very simply is God's "total package."

# ADDITIONAL NOTES

Use the following pages to complete the exercises addressed in the book. Should the paper not allow enough space, do so in a journal. You should use the book or another resource which is readily available as opposed to a notebook, as you may find that you need to rehash and peruse your writings in days to come.

♥ Describe the defining moment, as described in the book, and describe how it changed you.

_____

_____

_____

_____

_____

_____

♥ Find a scripture and write why you know the person(s) who hurt you was wrong. List why you know the offense was an injustice to your spirit and you as a woman.

_____

_____

_____

_____

_____

_____

♥ Write a letter of forgiveness. Use additional pages as necessary and list to your offender all of the reasons why you desire to forgive them. Do so in detail. Indicate in the letter in a general sense why you expect to benefit from this activity.

♥ Find three scriptures on forgiveness, and list them below.
Write down five reasons why your life will be better as a
result of giving mercy to your offender.

_____

_____

_____

_____

_____

_____

_____

_____

_____

_____

_____

♥ Write down the name(s) of the person who you intend
to share your action of forgiveness with. Let them know
you need for them to assist you in being accountable to
your emotions.

_____

_____

_____

_____

♥ Create your emotional resume.

_____

_____

_____

♥ Ask a person you trust what they think of you. Who do they believe you are? Ask them what others say of you. Make a decision to not be offended. List their responses below.

_____

_____

_____

_____

_____

_____

_____

_____

_____

_____

_____

_____

♥ Write your biography. Be sure to later type and put it in a place where you can readily reach it. Be sure to include all of your defining moments and your forgiveness actions to date. This biography should be a personal one and not professional. Be willing to define who you are and if you are able to add words like "loving, caring, and compassionate" be sure to do so. Your biography should be a statement of your triumphs over the hard areas of your life.

_____

_____

_____

_____

_____

_____

_____

_____

_____

_____

_____

_____

_____

_____

_____

_____

♥ Write down your faith plan. Your faith plan should include all of the actions you intend to take to assure your heart looks like the woman you desire to be. For every defining moment and offense which hardens you, you should have a corresponding action of faith which involves seed time and harvest time.

♥ Describe how your life will be different in the future as a
result of you embracing this process. For example: I will
have a woman whom I trust, who I will allow to give me
advice or correction. I will have more intimate relationships with my siblings. I will give potential male suitors
the benefit of the doubt rather than assuming their intent
is dishonorable.

I hope you will write me and share the good news of your new heart, the hope of your future relationships, and the peace of your present condition.

Contact Evelyn at:

EvelynWatkins.com